The Silliest
Joke Book Ever

By VICTORIA HARTMAN

Pictures By R.W. ALLEY

Lothrop, Lee & Shepard Books ◆ New York

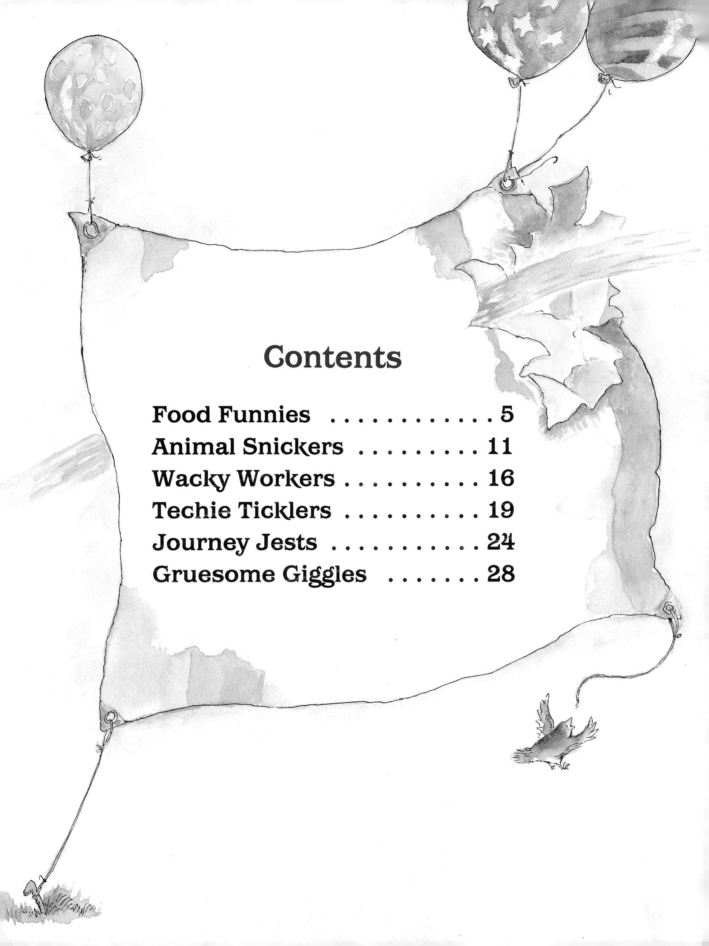

Contents

For Sara and Daniel Epstein
V.H.

For giggly Amy Dow
R.W.A.

First Edition   1 2 3 4 5 6 7 8 9 10

Library of Congress Cataloging in Publication Data
Hartman, Victoria. The silliest joke book ever / by Victoria Hartman ; pictures by R.W. Alley.
p.   cm.   Summary: A collection of riddle jokes on a variety of topics, including food, animals, and travel.
ISBN 0-688-10108-7.—ISBN 0-688-10110-0   1. Riddles, Juvenile. (1. Riddles. 2. Jokes.)   I. Alley, R. W.
(Robert W.), ill.   II. Title.   PN6371.5.H39 1993 818'.5402—dc20 92-22161 CIP AC

Food
Funnies

QUESTION:

What do you call a chicken
from outer space?

ANSWER:

An eggs-traterrestrial.

QUESTION:

What is the difference
between a skillet and a
nosey admirer?

ANSWER:

One is a frying pan,
the other is a prying fan.

QUESTION:

What kind of soda do Australian bears drink?

ANSWER:

Coca-Koala.

QUESTION:

What chocolate drink do owls like?

ANSWER:

Yoo Whoo.

QUESTION:

What do bugs drink?

ANSWER:

Apple spider.

QUESTION:

What kind of hamburger does an Eskimo like?

ANSWER:

A chilly-burger.

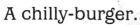

QUESTION:

Why couldn't the hamburger breathe?

ANSWER:

It was smothered with onions.

QUESTION:

What do you eat at a church supper?

ANSWER:

Hymn-burgers.

QUESTION:

Why was the hamburger afraid?

ANSWER:

He thought his past would ketchup with him.

QUESTION:

What cereal do gardeners hate?

ANSWER:

Weedies.

QUESTION:

Why was the hot dog so brave?

ANSWER:

He mustard up his courage.

QUESTION:

What's the favorite sandwich in the army?

ANSWER:

A drilled cheese sandwich.

QUESTION:

What kind of sandwiches did cavemen eat?

ANSWER:

Club sandwiches.

QUESTION:
How do sheikhs season their food?

ANSWER:
With sultan pepper.

QUESTION:
What kind of pasta do bullfighters like?

ANSWER:
Ravi-olé!

QUESTION:
What Egyptian queen liked spaghetti?

ANSWER:
Cleopasta.

QUESTION:
What food is good for your eyesight?

ANSWER:
See-food.

QUESTION:

How can you stop a
runaway coffee pot?

ANSWER:

With coffee brakes.

QUESTION:

What's the worst thing to
order at an ice cream
parlor?

ANSWER:

A hot sludge sundae.

QUESTION:

What pastry puts you
to sleep?

ANSWER:

A nap-oleon.

Animal Snickers

QUESTION:

What do Australian gossip columnists write?

ANSWER:

Kanga-rumors.

QUESTION:

What animal in Australia says cock-a-doodle-do?

ANSWER:

A kanga-rooster.

QUESTION:
What one-horned animal asks questions?

ANSWER:
A why-nocerous.

QUESTION:
When do bears go to the hospital?

ANSWER:
When they have a-panda-citis.

QUESTION:
How did the owl dry himself after a bath?

ANSWER:
With a hoot towel.

QUESTION:
What do sheep say at Christmas?

ANSWER:
Season's Bleatings.

QUESTION:
What do you call a happy dog?

ANSWER:
Satis-Fido.

QUESTION:

What do you call an
overactive snake?

ANSWER:

A hyper viper.

QUESTION:

What bunny gives out
parking tickets?

ANSWER:

Meter Rabbit.

QUESTION:

How do lizards work out?

ANSWER:

On newt-ilus machines.

QUESTION:

What extinct flying reptile
wore a crown?

ANSWER:

A tiara-dactyl.

QUESTION:

What kind of dinosaur
cried a lot?

ANSWER:

Tear-annosaurus.

Wacky Workers

QUESTION:

Why didn't the human cannonball go back to work?

ANSWER:

She was fired.

QUESTION:

What do you call a wandering detective?

ANSWER:

Sherlock Roams.

QUESTION:
Why did the astronaut smile when she got her paycheck?

ANSWER:
She got a cosmic raise.

QUESTION:
How does a lumberjack sign his letters?

ANSWER:
Yours treely.

QUESTION:
How do detectives hang up their laundry?

ANSWER:
With clues-pins.

QUESTION:
Who built Noah's boat?

ANSWER:
An ark-itect.

QUESTION:
What do you call a sailor who always says yes?

ANSWER:
An aye dropper.

QUESTION:
How do plumbers learn their occupation?

ANSWER:
On-the-job draining.

QUESTION:
Why did the shepherd think he was in jail?

ANSWER:
He was behind baas.

Techie Ticklers

QUESTION:

Where do Martians play video games?

ANSWER:

At meteor centers.

QUESTION:

What is a hockey player's favorite video game?

ANSWER:

Puck-man.

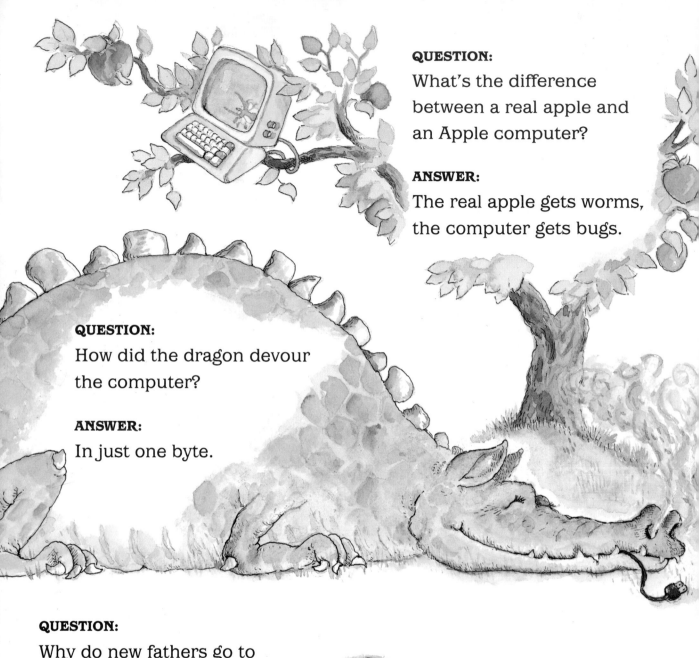

QUESTION:

What's the difference between a real apple and an Apple computer?

ANSWER:

The real apple gets worms, the computer gets bugs.

QUESTION:

How did the dragon devour the computer?

ANSWER:

In just one byte.

QUESTION:

Why do new fathers go to computer school?

ANSWER:

They want to learn da da processing.

QUESTION:

What do you say to a baby computer bug?

ANSWER:

Glitchy-glitchy-goo.

QUESTION:
Why did the girl dip her computer in caramel?

ANSWER:
She wanted a candied Apple.

QUESTION:
What does a shark have in common with a computer?

ANSWER:
They both have megabytes.

QUESTION:
What has 40 megabytes and 18 wheels?

ANSWER:
A Mac truck.

QUESTION:
Why did the runner take up computer graphics?

ANSWER:
He wanted to be a laser sprinter.

QUESTION:
How does an up-to-date shepherd tell time?

ANSWER:
With a digital flock.

QUESTION:
What do you call very little brides?

ANSWER:
Micro-wives.

QUESTION:
How does a rooster listen to music?

ANSWER:
With a Squawk-man.

QUESTION:
Why do parakeets go into electronics?

ANSWER:
They like molty-media.

QUESTION:
What do you hear from a happy video cassette recorder?

ANSWER:
VC Aaaaahs.

QUESTION:
What do you call an unshaven compact disc machine?

ANSWER:
A see-dy player.

QUESTION:
What kind of worm plays computer games?

ANSWER:
A video tape-worm.

QUESTION:
Why was the computer screen ready for New Year's Eve?

ANSWER:
It had good resolution.

QUESTION:
What do you call the steward on a computer engineer's flight?

ANSWER:
The byte attendant.

Journey Jests

QUESTION:

How did the lamb go into outer space?

ANSWER:

On a rocket sheep.

QUESTION:

Where do you go ice-skating in outer space?

ANSWER:

The rinks of Saturn.

QUESTION:

What did the mouse pilot say?

ANSWER:

This is your captain squeaking.

QUESTION:

Who helps ships come into the harbor?

ANSWER:

Buoy Scouts.

...THIS WAY...

...THIS WAY...

...THIS WAY!

QUESTION:

What did the rowboat say when it won the race?

ANSWER:

That was oar-some!

QUESTION:

What do an overturned boat and a hat measurement have in common?

ANSWER:

They are both cap-sized.

QUESTION:

Why did the horse go to Canada?

ANSWER:

He wanted to see Whinny-peg.

QUESTION:

What's the difference between a covered wagon and a dangerous gardener?

ANSWER:

One is a prairie schooner, the other is a scary pruner.

QUESTION:

What kind of rabbit can help change a flat tire?

ANSWER:

A jack rabbit.

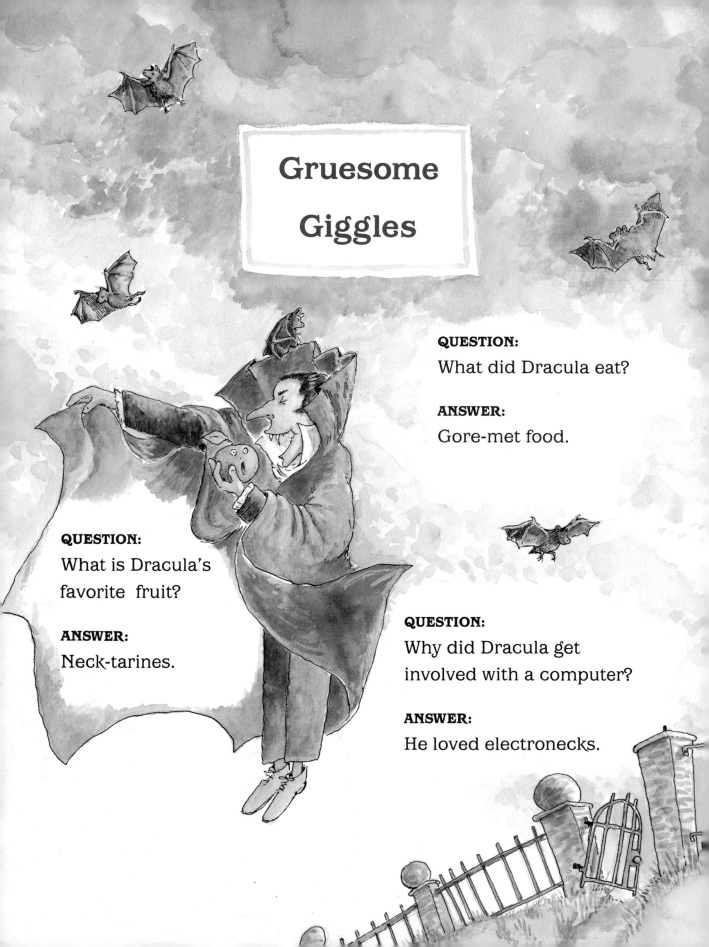

Gruesome Giggles

QUESTION:
What did Dracula eat?

ANSWER:
Gore-met food.

QUESTION:
What is Dracula's favorite fruit?

ANSWER:
Neck-tarines.

QUESTION:
Why did Dracula get involved with a computer?

ANSWER:
He loved electronecks.

QUESTION:
What do witches like for dessert?

ANSWER:
Scream puffs.

QUESTION:
Why was the ghost making so much noise?

ANSWER:
She was letting off scream.

QUESTION:
How do ghosts wash their hair?

ANSWER:
With sham-boo.

QUESTION:
How do you clean a cemetery?

ANSWER:
With ghost dusters.

QUESTION:
Why did the musician get mad at the mummy?

ANSWER:
She was singing out of tomb.

QUESTION:
What do mummies love to listen to?

ANSWER:
Wrap music.

QUESTION:
What do you call it when mummies get dressed?

ANSWER:
A wrap session.

QUESTION:
Why was the mummy so jumpy?

ANSWER:
He was all wound up.

QUESTION:
How do monsters watch scary movies?

ANSWER:
With video eeek-quipment.

QUESTION:
What do monsters do when they have a sore throat?

ANSWER:
Gar-goyle.

QUESTION:
How did the monster get around in the snowy mountains?

ANSWER:
It rode a blob-sled.

QUESTION:

How does a zombie get
to class?

ANSWER:

On the ghoul bus.

sweet dreams....

QUESTION:

What's covered with hair
and grants wishes?

ANSWER:

A furry godmother.